SCIENCE SUPERSTARS

LOUIS PASTEUR

Nancy Dickmann

Raintree is an imprint of Capstone Global Library Limited, a company incorporated in England and Wales having its registered office at 264 Banbury Road, Oxford, OX2 7DY – Registered company number: 6695582

www.raintree.co.uk
myorders@raintree.co.uk

Produced for Raintree by Calcium
Editors for Calcium: 3REDCARS
Designers for Calcium: Paul Myerscough and 3REDCARS
Originated by Capstone Global Library Limited © 2018
Printed and bound in India

ISBN 978 1 4747 5876 5 (hardback)
22 21 20 19 18
10 9 8 7 6 5 4 3 2 1

ISBN 978 1 4747 5883 3 (paperback)
23 22 21 20 19
10 9 8 7 6 5 4 3 2 1

British Library Cataloguing in Publication Data
A full catalogue record for this book is available from the British Library.

Acknowledgements
We would like to thank the following for permission to reproduce photographs:
Picture credits: Cover art by Mat Edwards; Dreamstime: Mike Kiev 45t, Konstantins Visnevskis 12c; Shutterstock: AlexanderJE 24c, Baloncici 20b, Catolla 32t, Chippix 23t, Arina P Habich 37t, Knorre 19t, Sergey Lukyanov 30b, Martynowi.cz 42c, Morphart Creation 16b, Motorolka 22b, Khomkrit Phonsai 29t, Pressmaster 44t, Promotive 34c, Smuay 17t, Toey19863 27t, Vasilyev 13b, Teri Virbickis 21t, John Wollwerth 31t; Wellcome Library, London: 6b, 7t, 9t, 10b, 11t, 14b, 25t, 35b, 36b, 38c, 40c; Wikimedia Commons: 39c, Fred Barnard/Illustrated London News 28c, Albert Edelfelt, Musée d'Orsay, Paris,15c, Wilhelm Fechner 33t, Ismeretlen 41t, Félix Nadar, Dibner Library of the History of Science and Technology 5c.

Every effort has been made to contact copyright holders of material reproduced in this book. Any omissions will be rectified in subsequent printings if notice is given to the publisher.

Contents

Chapter 1

Who was Louis Pasteur?

On the evening of 6 July 1885, a scientist sat in his laboratory in Paris, thinking hard. For the past several years he had been trying to find a vaccine that would prevent a terrible disease called rabies. He had finally succeeded in finding one that worked on dogs, though it had never been tested on humans. That day, a nine-year-old boy called Joseph Meister had been brought to his lab. Joseph had been badly bitten by a dog with rabies. There was no cure for the disease – Joseph was doomed to die a painful death.

The scientist did not know what to do – he had never experimented on a human being before. Using the vaccine might save the boy's life, but it might also harm him. Did he have the right to make that choice? He thought long and hard about it, and decided that he had to at least try to save the boy. He prepared a syringe of the experimental vaccine.

This scientist's name was Louis Pasteur, and he made the right choice that night. The vaccine worked and saved the boy's life. Soon, hundreds – then thousands – of other people were saved with the same vaccine. Even if that had been Pasteur's only achievement, we would still remember him. The rabies vaccine, however, was only one triumph in a glittering scientific career that included breakthroughs in food production, disease prevention and more.

STAR CONTRIBUTION

Life saver!

Few scientists have done more to improve the lives of humans than Pasteur. His work on fermentation helped make our food safer, and also saved the jobs of many people who worked in wine and beer production. His research into infectious diseases laid the framework for new generations of scientists, who have discovered ways to prevent and cure diseases that once killed millions of people.

First steps

Louis Pasteur was born on 27 December 1822, in the small French town of Dole. His father, Jean-Joseph Pasteur, was a tanner, whose job involved turning animal hides into leather. The family's tall, narrow house opened onto a canal, with the tannery in the cellar. The house was just one in a row of similar tanners' houses, where the strong smells of the chemicals used in their trade filled the air.

Louis was the Pasteurs' third child. Their first child had died as a baby. This was not uncommon. At the time of Pasteur's birth, many people, especially young children, died from infections or diseases such as cholera or typhoid. Doctors did not yet have a full understanding of how the human body worked, or how diseases were spread. Many people had no access to clean water. In fact, the canal outside the Pasteurs' house was probably filled with all kinds of dangerous waste, as well as the tanning chemicals.

A few years after Louis was born, his family moved to the nearby town of

As an adult, Pasteur often returned to the house in Arbois where he grew up. Today, you can visit it to see how he lived and worked.

Big ambitions

Pasteur's father was a fiercely patriotic Frenchman, who had fought in the French army. He wanted his son to have a better life than the one he had led. He did not want Louis to become a tanner, but he did not want him to be an artist, either. Louis' father thought that his son should get a good education and become a teacher at the local school.

SUPERSTAR FACT

Dole is in an area of forests and rolling hills. At the time of Pasteur's birth it had about 10,000 residents.The house where he was born is now a museum where visitors can learn about the story of his life.

Arbois. At school, Pasteur was just an average pupil, with no sign of being a scientific genius in the making. He was a very talented artist, though, and painted portraits of his family and friends.

pupil power!

In 1838, Pasteur went to school in Paris but was so homesick that he soon returned to Arbois. The following year he moved to a school in Besançon, about 50 kilometres (30 miles) away, where he was much happier. His classmates later remembered him as being very serious and focused on his work. Pasteur earned his Bachelor of Arts diploma in 1840, but the next year he failed the exam for a Bachelor of Science diploma. He kept studying hard and passed the following year, even though his chemistry grades were not good.

Pasteur decided to take the entrance exam for the École Normale Supérieure (ENS) in Paris, one of France's top universities. He passed the first part of the exam, but just barely. He did not want to enter the ENS as one of the lowest-ranked students, so he decided not to take the second half of the exam. Instead, Pasteur went back to studying. The next year he took the exam again and did much better – he had the fourth-highest score!

While Pasteur was waiting to take the entrance exam again,

SUPERSTAR STAT

Champion school

The École Normale Supérieure has been one of France's top universities for more than 200 years. It was originally founded to train teachers, but its students have included 13 Nobel Prize winners and 6 prime ministers of France.

he went to several lectures given by a famous chemist called Jean-Baptiste Dumas. At the time, Dumas was one of the greatest scientists in France, and he later became an important politician. After starting his career as an apothecary's assistant, Dumas became a pioneer in determining the atomic and molecular weights of various substances.

Pasteur was so interested in these lectures that he decided to study chemistry at university. He even took private lessons from Dumas' assistant. After several years of study at the ENS, Pasteur earned his degree in chemistry and physics. He then continued his studies as a graduate student and also took a part-time job as a laboratory assistant, working under the physicist Antoine-Jérôme Balard.

Chapter 2

Louis' early career

While he was at the ENS, Pasteur's abilities as a chemist were already attracting attention. In 1848, after earning his doctorate, he was appointed professor of physics at a high school in the city of Dijon. He was still only 25 years old. The following year he was offered an even better job, as professor of chemistry at the University of Strasbourg in eastern France.

Pasteur found more than just a satisfying job when he moved to Strasbourg. Here he met Marie Laurent, the daughter of the university's rector, and soon fell in love. They were married on 28 May 1849, and it turned out to be an excellent match. Marie was interested in science and often helped Pasteur with his work. She took part in his research and experiments, and became a valuable laboratory assistant.

This portrait shows Pasteur as a young man, when he was just beginning his career.

Acid tests

Tartaric acid has the chemical formula $C4H6O6$. This means that each molecule of tartaric acid has four atoms of carbon, six of hydrogen and six of oxygen. Their arrangement is what gives tartaric acid its unique properties. It is found naturally in some plants, and is one of the main acids found in wine. The acid is sometimes added to foods to give them a sour taste.

These were happy times for Pasteur. He and Marie eventually had five children – four girls and a boy. He was able to enjoy his growing family as well as make a name for himself with his scientific work. At the time of his marriage, Pasteur was focusing his research on two particular chemicals – tartaric acid and paratartaric acid. He made a number of trips to Germany, Vienna and Prague to visit factories that made the chemicals and to meet and share ideas with other scientists who were working on the same topic.

In addition to teaching, Pasteur was expected to continue with his research. It was at Strasbourg that he began his research into fermentation, though his big breakthroughs would come later.

Louis and Marie (above) had a long and happy marriage. She knew how important Pasteur's work was and made sure that he had time to do it properly.

Crystal studies

Louis Pasteur first came to the attention of the scientific world thanks to his work in crystallography. All substances are made up of atoms, and crystallography is the study of how atoms are arranged in crystals. Atoms are much too small to see, even with the most powerful microscopes, so scientists use other methods to learn about their structure. Knowing their structure is important because it helps to explain the properties of atoms.

A German chemist called Eilhardt Mitscherlich, had been studying two substances, tartrates and paratartrates, which had identical chemical properties. This means they were made up of the same numbers of atoms of different elements. Mitscherlich discovered that the two substances reacted differently to a certain type of light, but he could not explain why. Tartrates changed the angle of the light, but paratartrates did not. Mitscherlich was unable to understand how chemically identical substances could affect light in two different ways.

Wow!

Crystals come in many different shapes. For example, salt crystals are shaped like cubes.

Crystal opposites

Pasteur believed that the asymmetrical crystals were the result of living processes and, in a way, he was right. Many substances, including tartaric acid, can be found naturally or synthesized (produced) in a lab. Now we know that many of them show one type of alignment in the natural form and the opposite type in the man-made form.

STAR CONTRIBUTION

Pasteur began to study these substances and discovered that although they were made up of the same chemicals, their structure was different. Even more interesting was that the different structures of the crystals seemed to match up with their effect on the light. There were two main types of crystal, left-aligned and right-aligned, which were basically mirror images of each other. Pasteur discovered that a paratartrate had equal amounts of left and right crystals, and they canceled each other out, so that light was not affected when it passed through them.

This diagram shows how sodium and chlorine atoms are arranged in a lattice to form a salt crystal.

Salt   NaCl

● – Na
○ – Cl

Pasteur the scientist

Scientists today use the "scientific method." This means they make observations and ask questions, then formulate a hypothesis – a theory that might explain their observations. They test the theory and analyse the results before making conclusions. Pasteur was no different. When faced with a new problem or research question, he would study all the available data. He would look at the ideas proposed by other scientists, trying to find connections that others had missed. Then he would begin his own experiments.

Pasteur was incredibly patient and would spend days following up every clue, testing every aspect of his hypothesis and making careful notes. Sometimes he would discover something new that made him rethink everything he had done up to that point. Instead of being discouraged at having to start again, he would tackle the new challenge with enthusiasm.

Wow!

Many of Pasteur's great discoveries were made by studying substances under this microscope.

Be prepared!

One of Pasteur's most famous quotes was "In the field of observation, chance favours only the prepared mind." Sometimes an experiment might throw up an unexpected result. Some scientists might take this to mean that the experiment had failed, but a "prepared mind" – one that knew what to look for – would be able to see its significance.

Even though Pasteur was kept busy with his research, he took his duties as a teacher very seriously. After several years at the University of Strasbourg, he took a job as professor and dean at the new Faculty of Science at the University of Lille, in northern France. This was a more senior position, and he was able to make changes in the way things were done there. One of his biggest changes was to make sure that students did laboratory work. At that time, many universities taught science only through lectures. Pasteur believed, however, that hands-on experience was crucial for learning. He insisted on high standards and difficult exams, and on challenging students to do their absolute best. The students did not always like Pasteur's strict methods, but no one could argue with the successful results.

Pasteur would repeat experiments again and again to make sure the results were accurate.

Chapter 3

Fermentation fascination

While he was teaching at Lille, Pasteur organized visits to nearby factories, so that his students could see how chemistry was used in industry. Before long, a local businessman who owned a factory that produced alcohol from sugar beets approached him. Instead of alcohol, he was ending up with a substance similar to sour milk. The problem was costing the factory owner a lot of money.

The process that creates alcohol is called fermentation. In Pasteur's time people knew that leaving fruits or grains in covered containers for a long time produced wine and beer, and that milk eventually turned sour, but no one fully understood how fermentation worked. We now know that fermentation happens when a living thing converts a carbohydrate into alcohol or an acid. For example, tiny living things called yeast cause fermentation in beer when they convert sugar into alcohol. Cheese is produced when bacteria added to milk turn its sugars into lactic acid.

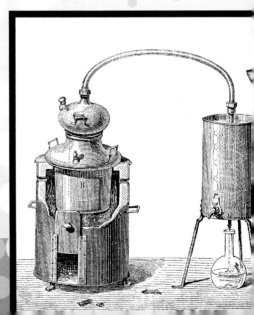

Spontaneous generation

Long ago, many people believed that life could be generated spontaneously. For example, they thought that fleas could be created from dust, or that maggots could appear instantly in dead flesh. Fermentation was seen as a type of spontaneous generation. Pasteur was determined to prove these ideas wrong.

SUPERSTAR FACT

In Pasteur's time, scientists could not agree on what caused fermentation. Many of them believed that it was a purely chemical process that did not involve living things. One famous scientist, Justus von Liebig, believed that, in the right conditions, oxygen could cause elements to rearrange themselves to form alcohol. He was wrong, but many scientists agreed with him at the time.

Ever since microscopes had been invented in the 1600s, scientists had been learning about the tiny living things they could see with these instruments. Some scientists had examined yeast under a microscope but did not realize until about 1835 that it was a living thing. Pasteur wanted to find out more about the role it played in fermentation.

Blame it on the microbes

Pasteur's experimentation with the spoiled alcohol soon led him to the discovery that there were two types of fermentation: alcoholic fermentation, which is caused by yeast, and lactic acid fermentation, which is caused by bacteria. After careful observation, Pasteur was able to see differences between yeasts and the smaller bacteria. He was convinced that these living organisms were the key to understanding and controlling fermentation.

Pasteur was eventually able to prove that fermentation could not take place without microorganisms, and that the process happened in the absence of oxygen. This seemed to go against the current belief that all life needed oxygen. Pasteur had discovered that some types of bacteria thrive without oxygen, and he made up a new name for them – anaerobes.

Not everyone agreed with Pasteur's new discoveries. As long as scientists still believed in spontaneous generation, they refused to accept his theories. In 1859, however, Pasteur decided to deal with the theory of spontaneous

STAR CONTRIBUTION

The Pasteur Effect

Pasteur noticed that bacteria near the edge of a microscope slide and exposed to oxygen were less active than those in the middle. He experimented by sending a current of oxygen-rich air through a liquid. He was amazed to see that the microorganisms stopped moving, and the fermentation process also stopped. This is now called the Pasteur Effect.

This picture shows the shape of the baker's yeast used for baking and for brewing beer. As part of its life processes, it turns sugars into carbon dioxide and ethanol.

generation once and for all. He took two identical glass flasks with S-shaped necks, filled them with beef-broth, and boiled the liquid to kill any microorganisms. In the first flask, the S-shaped neck trapped any particles from the air before they could reach the broth. It stayed clear, with no fermentation. Pasteur broke the neck off the other flask, so that air and other particles could get inside, and the broth soon turned cloudy. If spontaneous generation had been real, the broth in the curved-neck flask would have become cloudy too, because the germs would have spontaneously generated. Pasteur had proved that the spontaneous generation theory was wrong.

Pasteurization power!

Pasteur's fame was growing, and in 1863 the Emperor of France, Napoleon III, got in touch. The country's wine industry was in trouble, and the winemakers were desperate for a solution. Thousands of gallons of wine, produced by fermentation, were being ruined through what the winemakers called "sickness". A "sick" wine lost its aroma and flavour, turned sour and was ruined. Boiling the wine could prevent this problem, but the high temperature affected the flavour of the wine.

Pasteur examined the wine under a microscope and noticed that good wine contained yeast cells. When the wine turned sour, however, he could see many bacteria in it. The bacteria were producing lactic acid, which turned the wine sour. Once a wine had fermented, the yeast eventually died. When the bacteria were not present, the wine kept its flavour, but when the bacteria were allowed to multiply, they turned it sour.

Wow!

As well as killing the bacteria that make milk spoil, pasteurization, such as at this dairy, can also kill disease-causing bacteria.

Read the label

The discovery of pasteurization was a huge leap forward in food production. Without it, food and drinks spoil much more quickly. Read the labels on your food and you'll be amazed at how widely Pasteur's technique is used today. Milk, juice, butter, cheese, yogurt, eggs, wine and many other foods and drinks are routinely pasteurized.

STAR CONTRIBUTION

For hundreds of years, France has been famous for its fine wines. Hundreds of thousands of people made a living in the wine industry.

Pasteur knew that he needed to find a way to eliminate the bacteria without boiling the wine. In 1864, he discovered that heating the wine to a temperature of 50-60 °C (120-140 °F), for just a few minutes, killed the bacteria. Because this temperature was lower than when something boils, the process did not affect the flavour of the wine.

Still, not everyone was convinced. A wine's flavour becomes richer as it ages, and some people said that "pasteurization", as the process became known, would stop this from happening. Finally, after a cargo of pasteurized wine had been shipped successfully on a long journey through the tropics, with its flavour unaffected, the new technique was accepted.

Saviour of beer!

Several years after his success with the wine industry, Pasteur turned his attention to beer. He lived at a time when many people did not have access to clean drinking water and found it safer to drink beer instead. Beer was made by adding barley malt to water and letting it ferment, with hops added for flavour. Just like wine, however, beer had a tendency to go bad, especially if shipped on a long journey.

There were two main types of beer. "Brown" beer was brewed at a temperature of about 20 °C (70 °F), while "white" beer was brewed at a lower temperature. White beer also had to be stored at a low temperature, which was not easy in the days before refrigerators were invented. White beer kept better, but both types would eventually spoil.

Scientists often grow cells under controlled conditions – a process called culturing. It helps them to understand how microorganisms such as yeast and bacteria grow and reproduce.

Big business

When Pasteur started his research into wine and beer, France was producing about 4.9 billion litres (1.3 billion gallons) of wine per year, at a value of nearly £1 billion. In today's money, the value would be more than 20 times that. The wine industry was an extremely important part of the French economy.

Brewing in the 1800s was not an exact science. Brewers used the same methods they had used for hundreds of years.

After visiting breweries throughout England and France, Pasteur discovered that the yeast many brewers were using was contaminated. The other microorganisms mixed in with the yeast were causing the beer to go bad. Through careful research, he developed a way to keep the yeast pure and brew beer that would last.

In his work with wine and beer, Pasteur was not just concerned with finding a way to make drinks that tasted good. These industries were hugely important to the French economy, and thousands of people's jobs depended on their success. Pasteur was very patriotic, and he was also a humanitarian. He wanted his work to help people, such as by making their food safer or saving their jobs.

Chapter 4

The silkworm problem

While Pasteur was researching fermentation, the honours given to him were piling up. In 1862, he was elected to the Académie des Sciences, a group of France's top scientists. He was also offered a job at the École des Beaux-Arts in Paris, and so he moved to the city with his family. Pasteur was quickly becoming the expert scientist for any industry in trouble. That is why his former teacher, Jean-Baptiste Dumas, approached him in 1865 to help the French silk industry.

Silk can be dyed in a rainbow of colours, and it has been been used for hundreds of years to create beautiful garments.

Silk, first developed in China thousands of years ago, is an expensive, highly prized fabric that is soft, strong, light and beautiful. It is made from the cocoons of a particular type of insect, the silkworm. Silkworms are not actually worms – they are the young form of a type of moth. A silkworm makes its cocoon from a strong fibre that it secretes through its head.

Silk crisis

In 1853, the French silk industry produced 26,000,000 kilograms (57,320,000 pounds) of silk. Then the disease started to take its toll. By 1865, the yearly production was down to just 4,000,000 kg (8,820,000 pounds). The industry was on the brink of collapse.

SUPERSTAR STAT

Wow!

One silkworm cocoon contains about 1.6 kilometres (1 mile) of silk fibre. It takes about 3,000 cocoons to make 0.5 kg (1 pound) of raw silk.

The cocoons are boiled and unravelled, and the thread is made into fabric. The fabric is used not only for clothing but also for upholstery, rugs and bedding.

Silk had been produced in France since the 1400s, and by Pasteur's time it was one of France's most important industries. But a mysterious disease was killing the French silkworms. The silkworm breeders tried importing eggs from Italy, Syria, Greece, Turkey and elsewhere, but it seemed that all those silkworms were infected with the same disease. No one knew what was causing the disease, or how to stop it.

The same disease was causing problems for silk producers in other countries across Europe, as well as in China and Japan. It looked like it might be the end of the road for silk production.

Save the silkworms!

Pasteur did not know anything about the silk industry, and he had never studied infectious diseases before. Even so, he felt a duty to his country to try to help the silkworm breeders. As with all his research projects, he threw himself into it with complete dedication. Over the next five years, he became an expert silkworm breeder.

Pasteur's first step was to visit silkworm breeders all over France to find out more about their problems. He wanted to know if he was dealing with a single disease or a number of different diseases. Many breeders had noticed blotches on their silkworms' skin, a condition they called *pébrine*, from a southern French word for pepper. When examined under a microscope, the bodies of the affected silkworms

STAR CONTRIBUTION

Making predictions

In 1866, Pasteur examined 14 different colonies of silkworms in one town. He left a sealed envelope with the town's mayor that contained his prediction about which colonies would survive. At the end of the silk season, the mayor opened the letter. In 12 out of the 14 cases, Pasteur's prediction was correct. He had shown that the disease could be spotted in the unhatched eggs.

Pasteur spent months studying generation after generation of silkworms under his microscope. Eventually he discovered that by discarding the eggs infected with disease, silkworm growers could help their colonies recover.

were shown to contain tiny globules. But many healthy worms had them, too.

After much research, Pasteur concluded that the globules were actually tiny parasites. They entered the silkworm either with its food or through small wounds. Some infected moths could lay perfectly good eggs, while others laid infected ones. Pasteur eventually discovered that the silkworms infected early in their life cycle would lay infected eggs, but silkworms that were infected later in life would not.

During his research, Pasteur also discovered another disease, called flacherie. Silkworms suffering from flacherie had a bad smell, similar to fermenting mulberry leaves. Pasteur was able to pinpoint the cause of this disease as well.

Personal tragedy

Pasteur had become a hugely respected scientist, in great demand with universities and industry. But these were difficult times for him and his family. Louis and Marie Pasteur had five children, but in 1859 their oldest daughter, Jeanne, died at the age of nine. She had contracted typhoid fever, an illness caused by bacteria. It is usually passed on through the faeces of an infected person, and in Pasteur's time, when drinking water was not always clean, it was a common disease.

Pasteur was devastated by Jeanne's death. "I cannot keep my thoughts from my poor little girl, so good, so happy in her little life, whom this fatal year now ending has taken away from us," he wrote in a letter

The people of Paris rallied to fight the Prussians in 1870, but the city was surrounded and the Pasteurs were lucky to get out.

to his father. "She was growing to be such a companion to her mother and me, to us all." Worse, however, was yet to come. In 1865, Pasteur's father died, as well as his two-year-old daughter, Camille, who had suffered a liver tumour. Less than a year later, his daughter Cécile died of typhoid fever at the age of 12.

In 1868, while he was still working on the silkworm problem, Pasteur suffered a stroke. He was treated at home, with doctors using leeches in an attempt to cure him. His family were worried that he would not survive, but he slowly recovered. His left arm and leg, however, were permanently paralysed. After Pasteur's stroke, Marie's help with his work became even more important. Then, in 1870, France went to war with the state of Prussia. Pasteur and his family were forced to flee Paris as the Prussian army approached.

Chapter 5

Vaccination victories

In Pasteur's time, diseases such as cholera, typhoid and plague killed thousands of people each year. They could sweep through a city or town, infecting huge numbers of people. No one could agree, however, on how these diseases spread. For centuries, many people had believed that illness and disease were caused by natural imbalances in the body. For example, they treated some diseases by using leeches to suck out "impurities" in the blood. Also, many people still believed in the "miasma theory", which stated that particles from rotting organic matter caught in a poisonous vapour or mist – the "miasma" – caused disease if breathed in. This theory, however, by claiming that diseases were a direct result of contaminated water or poor sanitation, was not completely wrong.

Scientists in the 1800s were aware of microorganisms. In fact, as early as 1700 a French scientist called Nicolas Andry proposed that

Arrgh!

Many medical treatments in Pasteur's day, including the use of leeches to suck blood from people, were based on wrong ideas about what caused disease.

Diseases such as cholera, which causes vomiting and diarrhoea, can spread in places with poor sanitation.

Killer cholera

Diseases such as cholera were real killers. Between 1816 and 1826, a pandemic – which is a particularly bad outbreak of a disease – swept across Europe and Asia, killing hundreds of thousands of people. A second major outbreak in the 1830s and 1840s spread to the United States. In the 1850s, cholera killed more than 1 million people in Russia alone.

microorganisms (which he called "worms") were responsible for smallpox and other diseases. Just a few decades later, the English botanist Richard Bradley theorized that plague and other illnesses were caused by "poisonous insects" that could be seen only with a microscope. But these ideas were not widely accepted. Even many respected scientists still preferred the miasma theory.

Pasteur's work with silkworms had shown him that microorganisms could cause disease. The deaths of his daughters, as well as his first-hand experience of disease and infection among wounded soldiers in the war with Prussia, convinced him that this should be his next project. If he could work out how diseases were spread, he might be able to develop a way to prevent them.

Anthrax attack!

Louis Pasteur had trained as a chemist, not a doctor. Even so, in 1873 he was elected as a member of the prestigious Academy of Medicine. Although many doctors looked down on him for his lack of training, Pasteur began to visit hospitals regularly. He wanted to learn more about diseases that he suspected were caused by microorganisms. The first disease he tackled, however, was one that mainly affected sheep – anthrax.

Anthrax is a serious, highly contagious disease that has been around since ancient times. It commonly affects sheep and cattle, but it can also infect humans. In Pasteur's time, anthrax killed hundreds of thousands of people and animals each year. But there had just been a breakthrough.

STAR CONTRIBUTION

Germ theory

The discoveries of Pasteur and Robert Koch led to what is now called the "germ theory of disease". This theory states that microorganisms cause some diseases by invading other living things, called hosts, and growing and reproducing inside them. Pasteur and Koch had finally managed to prove that the miasma theory was wrong. Once scientists were on the right track, they made huge progress in identifying the causes of disease, and finding cures.

Sheep infected with anthrax can
sometimes stagger around or have
difficulty breathing. The disease is
usually fatal.

The German scientist Robert Koch had
identified the bacterium that caused anthrax,
although not everyone accepted this. Many scientists argued that the presence of this bacterium in
the blood of infected animals was a coincidence.

Pasteur was able to prove Koch's theory. He took blood from an infected animal and
managed to culture the bacteria found in the blood. This means that he put the bacteria into
a new liquid and was able to make them reproduce, over and over. For several months he grew
a colony of anthrax bacteria. Then he injected the bacteria into several animals, which all died.
Pasteur had proved that it was the bacteria, and not anything else found in infected blood, that
caused the disease.

Making vaccines

Finding the cause of anthrax was an important discovery, but it did not solve the problem affecting France's farmers. Pasteur needed to find a way to fight anthrax, either by discovering a cure or a vaccine. About 80 years earlier, an English doctor called Edward Jenner had discovered that people who had been infected with cowpox, a relatively mild disease, never caught smallpox, a related disease that was much more serious. By deliberately infecting people with cowpox, he was able to protect them from smallpox. This was the first vaccine – from *vacca*, the Latin word for cow.

Jenner had been lucky, because there was already a mild illness that was related closely enough to smallpox to make people immune. Pasteur's research showed that although animals that recovered from anthrax became immune to it, there was still a problem – no "mild form" of anthrax existed. Injecting anyone with anthrax bacteria would likely cause death. If Pasteur wanted to develop a vaccine, he had to find a way to make the bacteria weaker.

In addition to studying anthrax, Pasteur was also working on a disease called chicken cholera. A lucky accident in the lab had resulted in a weak

Attenuation

Pasteur spent years working on the theory of attenuation. This meant stretching the strength of a microorganism so thin that it became weak enough for the immune system to fight it off. Through this technique, Pasteur succeeded in finding an attenuated vaccine for anthrax.

STAR CONTRIBUTION

form of the culture that caused the disease. This weakened culture protected chickens from infection with chicken cholera. Pasteur realized that the same technique could produce vaccines for other diseases.

After a series of experiments, Pasteur had an anthrax vaccine that he was convinced would work. The next challenge, though, was a difficult one – he had to convince farmers to let him inject their animals with what could be a deadly disease.

Edward Jenner's work saved many lives. Later smallpox vaccines were even more successful, and the disease was eliminated.

Proving his point

On 5 May 1881, a large crowd had gathered at a small farm near the town of Melun. There were politicians, farmers, vets, doctors, chemists and many others in the crowd. They had all come to see the start of a public demonstration of Pasteur's anthrax vaccine.

Like all of Pasteur's experiments, this one had been carefully planned, so that there could be no doubt about the results. He had been given 60 sheep for the experiment, which he divided into two groups of 25 and one group of 10. The group of 10 sheep – the control group – would receive no treatment at all. Of the other two, one group would receive two doses of the anthrax vaccine, and the other would receive nothing. Then, two weeks later, those

Pasteur risked his reputation by injecting sheep with the anthrax vaccine, but it proved a big success.

SUPERSTAR STAT

Sheep survivors

Pasteur's vaccine had an immediate effect. The very next year, in one region alone, nearly 80,000 sheep were vaccinated. For the previous 10 years, approximately 9 per cent of sheep had died each year from anthrax. After Pasteur's vaccine, the death rate immediately dropped to 0.65 per cent.

two groups would be injected with a powerful anthrax culture.

Everything went according to plan. When the witnesses returned to the farm on 2 June, all the animals that had been vaccinated appeared to be in perfect health. Of the 25 animals that had not been injected, however, 22 had already died, and the remaining 3 died that day. The vaccine had worked!

Another part of the experiment was aimed at stopping the spread of anthrax. Pasteur wanted to show that sheep could catch anthrax by grazing on land where sheep that had died of anthrax were buried. Earthworms in the soil could bring anthrax spores – tiny pieces of dormant bacteria – from the dead bodies up to the surface, where other sheep ate them. Pasteur proved that burning the dead bodies, or burying them far from grazing land, could stop the spread of anthrax.

Rabies alert!

After the success of his anthrax vaccine, Pasteur was approached by a vet who wanted him to help find a cure for rabies, a terrifying disease spread by infected animals, usually dogs. A single bite from an animal with rabies would eventually lead to high fever, aggressive behaviour, fear of water and eventually death. There was no cure.

Pasteur believed that a microbe in an animal's saliva caused rabies, but he could not see it with his microscope. We now know that it is a type of virus,

In the days when there was no cure for rabies, the sight of a rabid dog could cause fear and panic.

which is incredibly small. Pasteur decided that the best chance of a vaccine was to attenuate the virus, in the same way that he had attenuated the anthrax culture. He started a series of experiments on rabbits and soon discovered that the rabies virus, although it is passed on through saliva, is also present in the body in the brain and the spinal cord.

Disease beater

Pasteur first tested his rabies vaccine on humans in July 1885, and news of its success soon spread. Using his vaccine, by the end of 1886 nearly 2,500 people from all over the world had been treated successfully.

SUPERSTAR STAT

Pasteur took the spinal cords from rabbits that had died from rabies. The spinal cords were full of the virus, but Pasteur found that drying these body parts in the air weakened the virus. The longer they dried, the weaker the virus got. He took a dog that had been bitten by a rabid dog and gave it a series of injections of the dried spinal cord, starting with the weakest form and then using stronger and stronger forms. The vaccine worked – the dog did not develop rabies symptoms.

Pasteur had been working on rabies for several years now and had at last found a way to prevent the disease in dogs. Would it work on humans? He vaccinated Joseph Meister, a nine-year-old boy who had been bitten – and waited. To his delight, the boy survived. A few months later, Pasteur tried the vaccine on another boy and was successful again.

Joseph Meister had been bitten badly on his hand and legs by a rabid dog. His mother brought him from Alsace to Paris in the hope that Pasteur could save him.

Chapter 6

Late life and legacy

Louis Pasteur had become more than a national hero – he was an international hero. Although some doctors still disagreed with his method of treating rabies, the evidence that he was right kept mounting up. Even though he had not trained as a doctor, Pasteur had succeeded where other doctors had failed.

Pasteur had not gone into science to become rich and famous. He wanted to help people and to find out more about the world around him. His work on wine, silk and anthrax had made him famous in France, but now his name was known around the world. Pasteur was given many awards and invited to join prestigious societies. Roads, buildings, stations and ships were named after him. His seventieth birthday, in 1892, was declared a national holiday in France, and in 1895 he was awarded the Leeuwenhoek Medal – the highest award for work in microbiology.

In 1886, when the rabies vaccine spread around the world, Pasteur was 64 years old. It had been nearly 20 years since the stroke that nearly

Pasteur's seventieth birthday was celebrated with a big party at the Sorbonne, Paris' top university.

Late in his life, this photo was taken of Pasteur, surrounded by children who had been saved from rabies by his vaccine.

Research reward

In 1995, to mark the centenary of Pasteur's death, the Institut Pasteur/UNESCO Medal was created. The medal is given out every other year to a scientist working in the fields of medicine, fermentation, agriculture or food, who has carried out research that has had a positive impact on human health.

killed him. Ever since that day he had been unable to smile, and he had a speech impediment. His left arm was weak, and he dragged his left foot as he walked. Over the years, Pasteur suffered a series of smaller strokes, and gradually the paralysis in the left side of his body got worse. Despite these health problems, he had kept working. But he was now an old man, and it was becoming harder and harder to do the work that he loved. After 1888, he started working less. On 28 September 1895, Louis Pasteur died at the age of 72.

Dynamic institute

One of the greatest honours awarded to Pasteur was the founding of an institute in his name. After the success of the rabies vaccine, he wanted to set up an establishment devoted to fighting rabies. Donations came in from around the world, including one from the Russian emperor, Alexander III, after Pasteur's vaccine had saved Russian peasants' lives.

The Institut Pasteur was founded on 4 June 1887, and had its official opening on 14 November 1888. Pasteur was closely involved with it, and wanted it to be a centre for scientific research into infectious diseases. He was determined that the Institut's research should have practical applications that would help improve lives. He brought in scientists from France and other countries.

It did not take long for the Institut to start producing results. The year it was opened, two of its scientists discovered the cause of the disease diphtheria. A few years

In 1983, scientists at the Institut Pasteur were the first to isolate human immunodeficiency virus (HIV), the virus that causes acquired immune deficiency syndrome (AIDS). They were awarded the Nobel Prize in 2008 for their discovery.

A debt repaid

Joseph Meister, the first person to be treated with the rabies vaccine, was incredibly grateful to the man who had saved his life. As an adult, he served as caretaker at the Institut Pasteur until his death in 1940, at the age of 64.

SUPERSTAR FACT

later the cause of bubonic plague was identified. Over the next century, the Institut's scientists made important breakthroughs on polio, typhus, yellow fever and many other diseases.

Today, the Institut Pasteur is one of the world's leading medical research centres. It has expanded from its original home in Paris, and it is now a global network of 32 institutes and 130 research units around the world. More than 2,600 people work in the Paris headquarters alone, many of them dedicated to solving medical problems in the developing world.

In recent years, scientists at the Institut have made even more breakthroughs such as developing a test for detecting colon cancer and a test for diagnosing stomach ulcers.

Pasteur's legacy

Louis Pasteur had a huge impact on the modern world. He developed pasteurization, the process that we still use to make our milk safe and to prevent beer, wine and other foods from spoiling. He made important advances in the study of crystals, his work with silkworms rescued an entire industry, and the vaccines he developed saved countless lives.

His greatest contribution to the world is probably his work on the germ theory of disease. Pasteur was not the first person to develop this theory, but his work finally proved it to the world. Knowing how diseases were caused and spread was a huge leap forward in medicine. Ever since then, it has allowed scientists around the world to find cures and treatments for a huge number of diseases.

As a scientist, Pasteur was careful, patient and very precise. He had a logical

STAR CONTRIBUTION

Appliance of science

In Pasteur's time, the winemakers, silkworm breeders, and farmers carried out their work without understanding the scientific principles behind it. Pasteur showed them that applying science could solve many of their problems. Now these industries have their own laboratories and are constantly finding new ways to improve their processes.

Thanks to vaccines, children born today have a much better chance of surviving to adulthood than Pasteur's own children did.

Wow!

Scientists today have the benefit of advanced technology, but they still follow the same scientific method that Pasteur used.

mind and approached each new problem in the same way: examine the evidence, form a hypothesis, plan an experiment and analyse the results. If it did not work, he would go back and try something else. No detail was too small to be noted and analysed, and his careful notes made it possible for other scientists to build and expand on his work. As a teacher, Pasteur passed these methods on to his students, training the next generation of scientists.

Pasteur insisted on finding practical applications for his research. He could have become rich by patenting his discoveries, but he chose not to. He was not in it for the money – he wanted his work to help people. And he succeeded! In the century since Pasteur died, millions of people have lived safer, healthier lives as a result of his work.

Glossary

anthrax serious disease that affects sheep, cattle and other animals, and can also affect humans

asymmetrical being different on each side

atom smallest possible unit of a substance

attenuation process that makes a disease-causing virus or bacteria weaker, so that it has a less powerful effect

bacteria tiny organisms that live in soil, water or the bodies of living things. Some bacteria cause disease, but others are important for many natural processes.

carbohydrate energy-giving substance found in food that is made out of carbon, hydrogen and oxygen

cholera deadly disease that can affect the digestive systems of humans and other animals

contagious able to be passed easily from one living thing to another

control group group in an experiment that cannot be affected by what is being tested

crystallography study of crystals and their structure

culture grow bacteria or other microorganisms in a laboratory, making them reproduce in order to study them

elements substances, such as iron, carbon or oxygen, that cannot be separated into any other substances

fermentation chemical reaction in which substances are broken down and energy is released

humanitarian person who wants to help people and make their lives better

hypothesis theory or possible answer to a scientific question

infectious diseases diseases or illnesses, such as chicken pox, that can be passed from one person to another

laboratory place where science experiments and research are carried out

lactic acid chemical that can be produced by some types of bacteria. It is what makes milk go sour.

microorganisms tiny living things that can only be seen with a microscope, including bacteria and viruses

microscopes scientific instruments that magnify objects so that they appear much bigger

molecule smallest unit of a substance that has all the properties of that substance

oxygen gas with no colour or smell and that is part of the air around us

parasites living things that make their home in or on another living thing

pasteurization process in which a liquid, such as milk or wine, is heated to kill any microorganisms living in it

patenting obtaining a legal document that gives the discoverer of a process or invention the right to be the only person to make and sell it

rabies deadly disease spread by animals that causes damage to the nervous system and is usually fatal

scientific method process used by scientists to make new discoveries

stroke damage to the brain caused by lack of blood flow, which can lead to problems with movement and speech

typhoid fever serious disease, also known simply as typhoid, caused by bacteria transmitted in contaminated food or water that can lead to high fever, diarrhoea, and often death

vaccine small amount of a disease that is used to prevent a patient catching the disease

virus tiny microbe that can cause disease

Find out more

Books

Louis Pasteur (Science Biographies), Nick Hunter (Raintree, 2014)

Micro-organisms (Essential Life Science), Richard and Louise Spilsbury (Raintree, 2014)

Modern Medicine (Medicine Through the Ages), Chris Oxlade (Raintree, 2012)

Science: A Children's Encyclopedia, Chris Woodford and Steve Parker (DK Children, 2014)

Websites

Learn more about 19th-century knowledge of the body and disease, at:
www.bbc.co.uk/schools/gcsebitesize/history/shp/modern/
indrevknowledgerev2.shtml

Discover more about Edward Jenner's life and work, at:
www.bbc.co.uk/schools/primaryhistory/famouspeople/edward_jenner

Find out more about Louis Pasteur's life and work, at:
www.dkfindout.com/uk/science/famous-scientists/louis-pasteur

Index